TECHNICAL ANALYSIS
FOR FOREX EXPLAINED

WAYNE WALKER

Table of Contents

INTRODUCTION

Congratulations on your personal copy of *Technical Analysis for Forex Explained*. This book will ensure that you are equipped to begin using technical analysis for forex trading and execute the strategies that go along with it. We will also examine several technical analysis indicators that can increase your profit making ability.

The book is primarily about technical analysis, however technical analysis does not operate in a vacuum, there are several other factors at play when you are trading. We begin with a brief review of the forex market since this book is technical analysis for forex (*if* you know everything there is to know about forex you can skip the first few pages and go direct to the technical analysis section).

The final chapters explore strategic trading tactics that you can begin using immediately, along with a section on making the transition from demo to live trading. The transition section has proven itself to be beneficial to traders of all types, from newbies to the more experienced who have been trading for some time. For those in a hurry, the Technical Analysis Quick Trade Guide, also in the later chapters, can have you trading almost right away.

Many of the quick trade techniques have been used by my past students to win the Nordic Trading Competition in Europe.

There are plenty of books on the market, thanks for choosing this one.

CHAPTER 1

FOREIGN EXCHANGE

What is forex? Or as many people call it FX, it is the world's most liquid market with a daily turnover of over 4 trillion US. Now if this number is 4.4 trillion or 4.5 trillion it is not so important to get caught up on that, the point to get is that a lot of people are trading forex. This is by far the most liquid market in the world, there is no close second. For example, a day of foreign exchange is roughly 2 to 3 months of trading volume on the New York Stock Exchange (NYSE).

It is OTC traded, indicating that there is no central exchange. This term OTC means over-the-counter, which implies that the parameters, the rules of how you trade are determined by your counterpart, there is no central body, there is no center of FX. As far as the trading, it is 24/5, from Sydney 5AM Mondays to New York 5PM on Fridays. For many people this twenty-four hour component is a plus, because in contrast to other markets, for example the equity market which has trading hours that are usually only from nine to five, eight to four, or eight to five depending on the country. If you are working or running a business then having the option of trading either before or after work is a plus, and this is another of the attractions that foreign exchange has for many people.

The forex centers and participants

In regard to where the volume is coming from, the bulk of it is from London, New York, Tokyo, Singapore, plus France and Germany which are now part of the Euro zone. Switzerland, Hong Kong, and Australia fills out the rest of the major currencies. Then you have the exotics which are about 18% of the market. This is where you will see a lot of what we call the minor currencies and some of the exotics. For example, the Danish Kroner, Swedish Kroner, Iraqi Dinar, Israeli Shekel are in this group. For our focus, it will be on the US Dollar, Euro, Sterling, Yen, and the Swiss Franc, not so much on the minor currencies. However, it is not a rule or an attempt to suggest that you should not trade those minor currencies, because if you are from those countries or if you have studied them or you have some reason why you are quite familiar with them, then sure you can go ahead and consider them. Outside of these reasons I would suggest that you really want to focus on the major currencies.

Commercial Banks

They provide dealing for their clients and they will also have proprietary traders who speculate with their banks' funds. This simply means traders who really trade with the bank's money. Many people working at a bank will have the title of trader, but what they are doing is what we call executing trades. For example, at a bank that I worked for, one of the things I did was execute trades as a member of an execution team. If a client wanted to place a trade by calling in with the request, "I want to buy ten million Eurodollars", I would buy it for him.

Hedge funds are also players in the market to invest and speculate. However, keep in mind that to have access to most hedge funds you will need to be classified as an accredited investor (200K USD in income or 1 million USD in assets outside of your primary residence).

Private Speculation

Then you have of course the private traders, you, me, and all the others. You will also have everyday transactions, this is with the physical forex (paper money). The focus of the technical analysis in this book will be on what we call the speculative foreign exchange, which is on price movements, but the two markets, the speculative and the actual physical paper money foreign exchange worlds do meet price wise.

EUR / USD since 1999

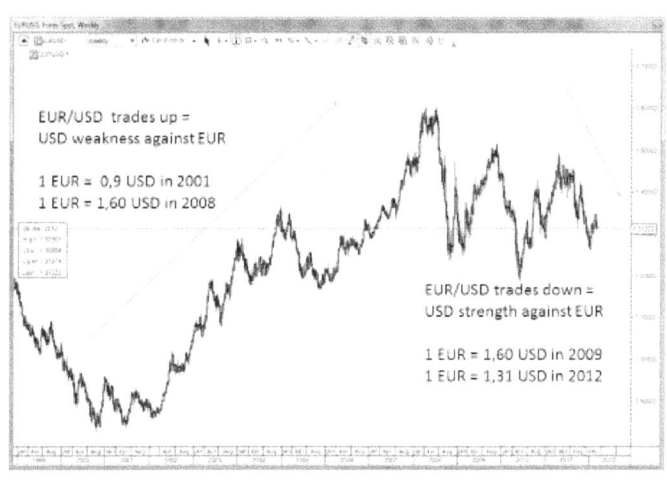

(Eurodollar movements since 1999)

For example with Eurodollar, when the Euro first came out, for one Euro, you would have received ninety cents in 2001, so in plain terms the Euro was weaker than the Dollar back then. Fast forward to 2008 a complete different story, the Euro was significantly stronger than the Dollar. Of course things can change, 2012 Eurodollar was trading at 1.31 and actually it is trading even lower now. This is the speculative foreign exchange, price movements.

INVESTOR IN EUROPE BOUGHT A HOUSE IN FLORIDA:

BOUGHT IN 2001:
PRICE USD 500.000 = EUR/USD 0,9000   EUR 555.555   USD declined
                                                            44% against the EUR from
SOLD IN 2008:   2001 to 2008
PRICE USD 500.000 = EUR/USD 1,6000   EUR 312.500

Now with the physical market, the worlds do need to meet. As seen in the visual above, we use the example of a person in Europe buying a home in Florida to illustrate when the Euro came out in 2001. Our buyer purchased the house priced at a half million dollars, but because the Euro was weaker than the Dollar they had to pay a premium. In this case they paid five hundred and fifty five thousand in Euros in order to get that house. In 2008 because the Dollar fell, that same house that was for a half million plus in Euros they could have bought it for three hundred and twelve thousand Euros. Huge difference! and this is where, as mentioned, the speculative foreign exchange and the physical world do need to meet.

What actually moves this market?

Rumors, economic data and reports, unfortunate things like war, terrorism, are never nice but they do have an influence on the market. There is a mini-fundamental analysis section later in the book for you to read further.

Why trade FX?

Definitely it is the ability to go long or short as we call it. Long means that we are buying, this is what most of us are familiar with. You buy something trading at one Euro, you sell it at three, four, or five. Most are comfortable with this, this is what we have been raised on, trading wise. Now with foreign exchange there is the short side. For example, you can sell something trading at a hundred dollars and if it falls to fifty, that's great, then you pocket the fifty dollar difference.

Next is the relatively low correlation to other asset classes, foreign exchange is foreign exchange, personally and for other traders, it is simply another asset class, it is not the best thing to trade, it is not the worst, it is another way to be in the market. For example, you have the other asset classes, commodities, real estate, government paper or bonds, forex is simply another one.

Why Trade FX?

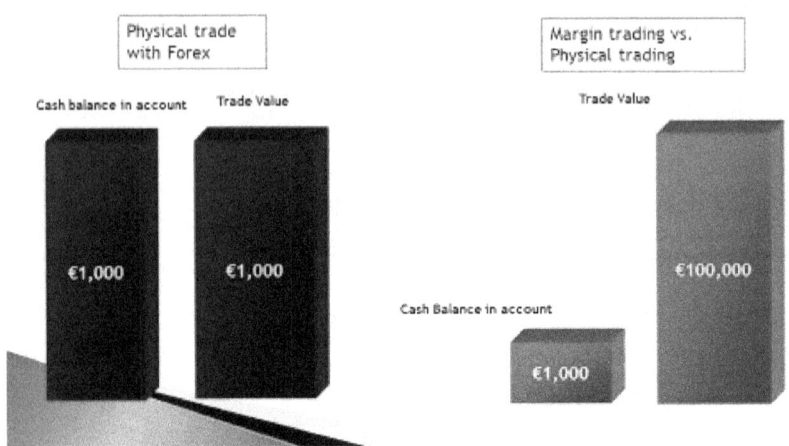

(Difference between physical and speculative forex)

In regard to the physical trade, taking a look at our chart above, on the left you have a cash balance of a thousand Euros, the most that you can actually take out(market exposure) in the market is a thousand Euros, this is on the physical one to one forex, or if you were trading physical stocks it is the similar concept. What we will deal with is on the right, margin trading. Some people call it gearing, you will also hear the term leveraging and it is trading "as if."For example, if you have a thousand Euros, you can take out a position of a hundred thousand Euros or more depending on your broker and what that means is that you can make a profit *as if* you have a hundred thousand Euros and you can also take a loss *as if* you have a hundred thousand Euros. Obviously with this type of leveraging, risk management is key. This is where three way orders can come into play to assist with risk management.

Some basic terms

Base currency: This is your exposure and this is also the currency that is traded.

Variable currency: This is how your profit and loss or P and L is calculated. For example with Eurodollar, the base currency is Euro and the variable is Dollar.

Basic FX terms

› EURUSD 1.5800
  1 EUR=1.5800 USD

› The Spread(Bid–Ask)

› Bid–Ask
  1.5800–1.5802
  0.0002(2 pips)

(Eurodollar at 1.5800, means that for one Euro you receive 1.58 Dollars)

The spread: Is the difference between the bid and ask price, this is how the banks make their money. We have the bid price 1.5800 on the left, this is the price you will receive when it's time for you to sell. On the right, the ask 1.5802, this is what you will need to pay when you want to buy. In this example we have a two pip spread and this is what your bank or broker will keep as income for themselves.

Basic review

If you are long you are buying, going long at fifty then you want the price to go up to fifty-one, fifty-two or higher. If shorting you are selling and you need the price to fall, going short at fifty you need the price to fall under fifty to profit. And if you are square, it means you have no market exposure, your positions are closed. To close a long position of a half million Eurodollars, you will need to sell a half million Eurodollars. That will remove your exposure.

More basic terms

Cable (GBPUSD): Is Sterling against the Dollar and this you will hear quite a bit amongst traders.
Swissy (CHF): The Swiss franc
Aussie (AUD): The Australian dollar
Kiwi (NZD): The New Zealand dollar
Loonie (CAD): The Canadian dollar
ZAR: The South African Rand
RUB: The Russian Ruble
Zloty (PLN): The Polish Zloty

"The figure": Means that it is all zeros at the end of the quoted price. In a quoting situation instead of saying one point two zero zero zero(1.2000), in a dealing room you would say one point two the figure.

Stop out: Indicates that your positions have been closed, all of them, and you will be in a stop out situation if you do not have enough funds to cover the margin requirement of your open positions.

CHAPTER 2

PRACTICAL TECHNICAL ANALYSIS

The key point to making money with technical analysis is identifying the trend and trading along with it. Trends reveal to you where prices are most likely to head in the future. If the trend of a currency pair is heading up, then you need to buy the currency pair to make money. If the trend of a currency pair is beginning to go lower, you need to sell the currency pair to profit. If the trend of a currency pair is sideways, with no clear direction, you either need to place contingent orders (not trades) or wait until a clear trend up or down is established before trading. It is not recommended to fight the trend, if you elect to do so, in most cases it will be an expensive experience for **you**.

Trends do not normally move straight up or straight down in a direct fashion. They usually move in one direction for a period of time and then temporarily retrace(reverse) part of the previous movement before continuing back on the original direction. Every time a currency pair retraces and begins moving in the opposite direction, it forms a new high or a new low. For example, with forex, new highs form when a currency pair moves higher and then turns around and moves lower. New lows form when a currency pair moves lower and then turns around and moves higher. Identifying these highs and lows allows you to identify whether a currency pair is in an uptrend, a downtrend or a sideways trend.

Uptrends - Markets that are trending upward form a series of higher highs and higher lows.

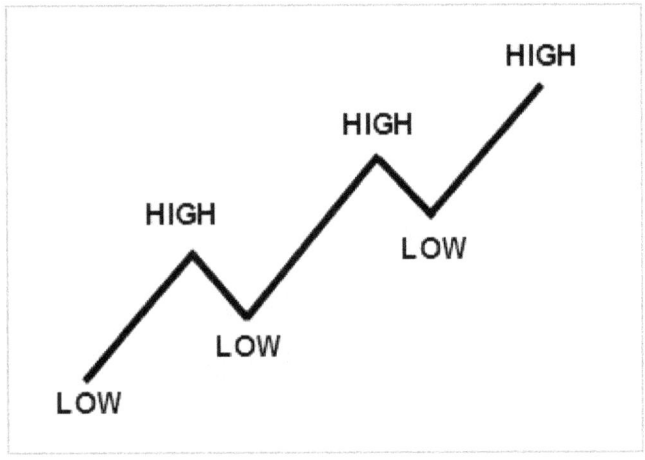

Downtrends - Markets that are trending downward form a series of lower highs and lower lows.

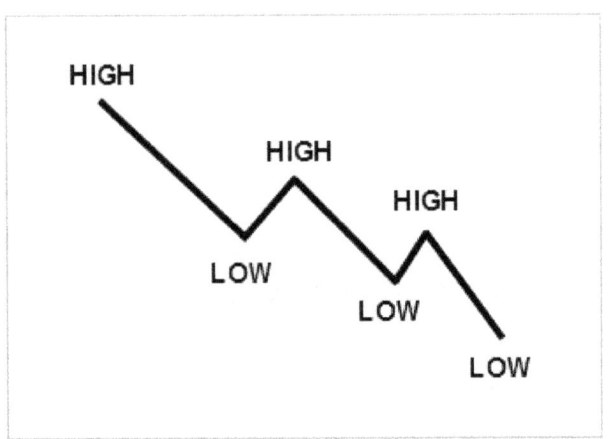

Sideways trends - Currency pairs that are trending sideways form a series of highs that are at approximately the same price level and a series of lows that are at approximately the same price level.

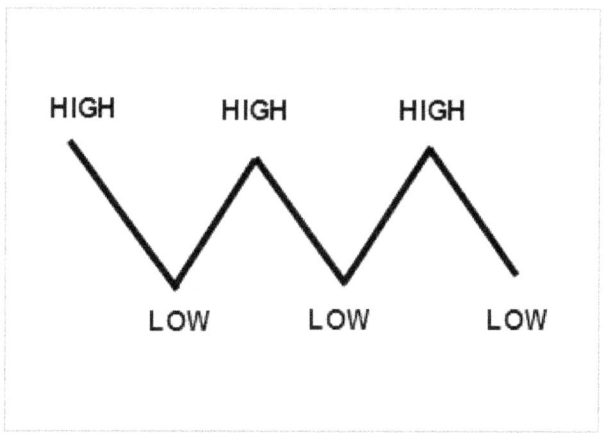

Trends - Whether they are uptrends, downtrends or sideways trends - can form over various time periods. Identifying the following trends over each time frame and being able to align them in your analysis is crucial to your success as a Forex trader.

Defining a candlestick chart

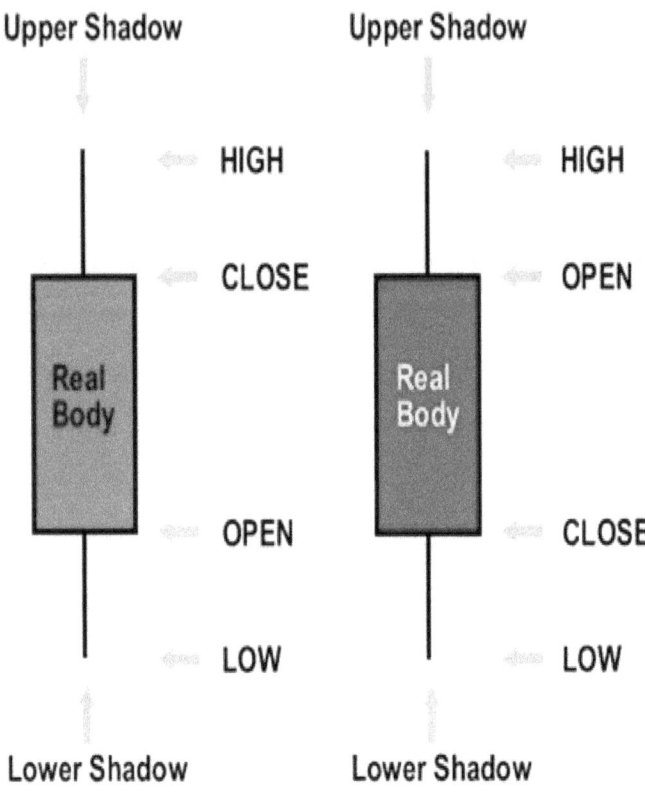

Let us begin by defining a candlestick. A candlestick is a line on a chart which represents one point and shows the high, low, open and close for each period.

For example, if we have a daily chart, each candlestick represents one day and will show the high, low, open and close for that day. On many platforms, a red candlestick means that the close price is lower than the open price for that period. A green candlestick means that the close price is higher than the open price for that period.

CHAPTER 3

TECHNICAL ANALYSIS INDICATORS

We will take a look at the Moving Averages, RSI and Bollinger Bands indicators.

First is the Moving Averages, and they are useful because they make it easier to spot a trend. This is key with foreign exchange or some of the other derivatives where an up market is good and a down market is also good. Therefore, all we need to do is to identify or spot this trend. To illustrate, a fifty day moving average adds up the closing prices for the last fifty days, divide by fifty and plots a point on the chart for each day.

Moving Average Chart :

Let us review some basic settings with the moving average indicator. If we have settings (on chart above) of MA ten, MA fifty, then ten is the short term, fifty is the long term. The shorter moving average, if that is above the longer, the trend is considered upward. If the shorter moving average is below the longer moving average, then the trends is considered downward. On a chart if you see that the ten is breaking beneath the fifty, the long term in this example, that could be taken as the initial sign of a sell signal.

With moving averages the buy and sell signals are generated by the price crossing above or below the moving average line. There is a term that you will hear a lot if you are around technical analysis folks, it is called the *golden cross* and it means that the short term breaks above the long term. The example we have is ten and fifty, but it could have been twenty and thirty, fifteen and seventeen, it depends on the trader and the instrument that they are trading.

Relative Strength Index

RSI graph is visible beneath the EURUSD chart.

The RSI, which is the Relative Strength Index is used to identify if the market (stock, currency pair, etc.) is overbought or oversold. It has an index from zero to one hundred. The RSI matches more or less what is happening on the chart and it should. Readings below thirty indicate that the market maybe oversold and when you see or hear the term oversold it mean excessive selling. Readings above seventy indicate that the market maybe overbought, excessive buying. Keep in mind these are indications, they are not guarantees of anything. As a note, the market can remain overbought or oversold for a considerable period of time. The RSI is a leading indicator, it begins giving signals before the trend has begun.

Bollinger Bands

Bollinger Bands are a tool that many investors and traders use when they want to add different technical analysis aspects to the trades that they have open. They are used to measure market volatility. The bands define the upper and lower limits of the trading range. When you view the bands on a chart(shown above), you will have a top and a bottom band, the space between the top and the bottom, many people call this the buy - sell channel. You use the space between the bands to get an idea of where you are within the trading range. If you are near the top, you know that you are close to the resistance level and there is a potential for a price reversal (the market changes direction). If you are at the bottom, you know that you are near the support level for a potential price reversal there. For the most part prices do remain between the bands. If the price begins to break out, people take this as a signal so you do need to be aware of that.

Understanding Support and Resistance Levels

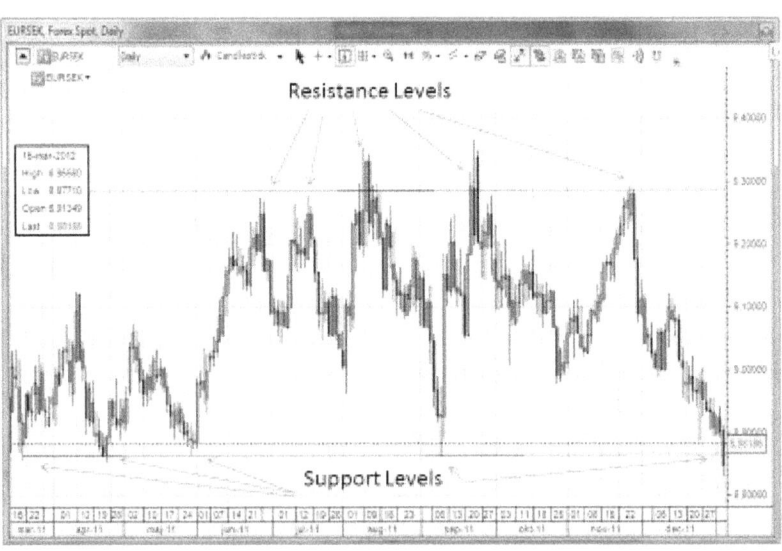

Support level is the price level at which the instrument traded has historically had difficulty falling below. For example if we have support around 1.4380, you would be able to see on a chart that the market has been to that level (1.4380) several times without falling lower, so in technical analysis jargon this would be considered a support level.

Resistance level is just the opposite, the price level at which the instrument has historically had difficulty trading above.

Chart patterns similar to the letters M & W

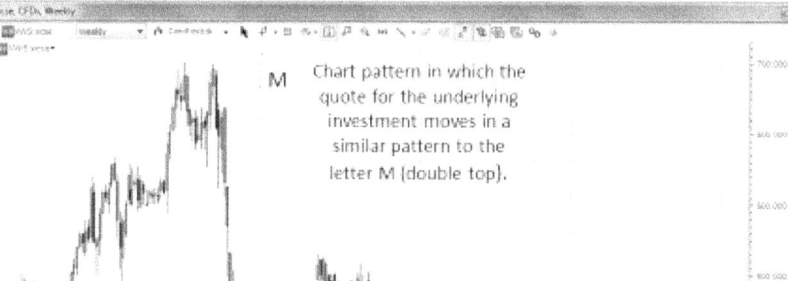

Chart patterns "W" double bottom or "M" double top

Chart patterns in which the price quoted for the underlying instrument moves in a pattern similar to the letter "W" (double bottom) or "M" (double top). Double top and bottom analysis are used in technical analysis to explain movements in a security or other investments, and can be used as part of a trading strategy to exploit recurring patterns. A double top and a double bottom are both trend reversal patterns.

A **double bottom** tends to occur after a strong downtrend, and it indicates that an uptrend may be imminent. The "bottoms" are valleys which are formed when the price hits a certain support level that cannot be broken. After hitting this level, the price will bounce off it slightly before returning to test the level again. If the price bounces off the support a second time, then you have a double bottom formation. If the second bottom cannot break the low of the first, then this is a strong signal that a reversal is going to happen. A 'neckline' is drawn at the high between the two 'bottoms'. With a double bottom, you could think of placing your long entry order above the 'neckline' because you are expecting the trend to change upwards.

A **double top** is usually formed after there is an extended uptrend, and it indicates that a downtrend may be imminent. The "tops" are peaks which are formed when the price hits a certain resistance level that cannot be broken. After hitting this level, the price will bounce off it slightly, but then return back to test the level again. If the price bounces off of that level again, then you have a double top. If the second top cannot break the high of the first top, then this is a strong signal that a reversal is going to happen. A 'neckline' is drawn at the low between the two 'tops'.

With a double top, you could think of placing your short entry order below the 'neckline' because you are expecting the trend to change downwards.

CHAPTER 4

TECHNICAL VS. FUNDAMENTAL ANALYSIS

We now examine the difference between technical and fundamental analysis. This is a topic where there has been quite a bit of debate particularly with traders. You will have the technical fans in one corner, then you have the fundamental fans in another and everyone is fighting over which method is the best. Let us review them on their individual merits.

Technical analysis means that you are using technical analysis indicators, for example moving averages, which helps you to identify the trend, and maybe another of the indicators for example the RSI (Relative Strength Index) to see if the market is overbought or oversold.

Fundamental analysis, this is when you take into consideration, for example, if taking a look at the stock market, the directors trading, the company's market share, what's in the product pipeline, P/E ratio, etc. These areas are relevant when you are looking to invest in stocks. For the people that are whom we call fundamental traders, they basically stick with this type of analysis and say this is the best way to arrive at a trading decision. My take on it and my colleagues view on this is that it really depends. When I say depends, I mean on your time frame.

Let us say you are a day trader, day traders open and close their orders or trades on the same day. Or you can go to the extreme which is called scalping, and amongst scalpers you will also have persons that are classified as extreme scalpers, they will have positions open from one or two seconds to maybe a minute. And with those traders, when they are in this type of aggressive trading, using fundamental analysis about company market share and product development, won't really help them that much because the time frame is only a couple of seconds. But if we go to the other side, and you are in this investment time frame, for me, investment would include investors that prefer to hold positions or take on a trade that will last anywhere from a year, out to two, three, or even five years. Then if you are investing, paying attention to fast changing one minute charts or other short term technical analysis tools is unwise, those are not really applicable. In reality there is not this competition between technical or fundamental, what I say is it really boils down to your time frame. Once you decide what your time frame is then you will use the appropriate tools. If you intend to do short term trading, your primary tool will be technical analysis, but if you have a longer time frame then you are looking more at fundamental analysis because with this longer time horizon you will need more data.

Economic Calendar (a fundamental analysis appetizer)

We will take a quick look at the market reports that matter the most. Central banks, CPI, Nonfarm payrolls, Housing Starts.

Central Banks: We have the FOMC, BOE, ECB. The market pays very close attention to these meetings, primarily through the Federal Reserve and its Federal Open Market Committee-FOMC. Clearly, the Bank of England-BOE, European Central Bank-ECB, are also very important reports and meetings that we pay attention to. They meet once a month to determine the monetary policy of their particular currency. Lately there has been a lot of focus towards the People's Bank of China, because obviously that particular bank now has quite a bit of influence within the financial markets.

Why should we care? The changes in these interest rates, will affect everything from financing, to bonds, definitely the stock market but the key for these reports or any of the economic reports is that whether those decisions are made differently from what the market expected. So for example, if there were an expectation of a 25 basis points cut in the interest rate and then when announced, it is a cut of 25 basis points, you might see some market movements but nothing all that dramatic should happen because that cut was already priced in the market. If it turns out that we expect a 25 basis points cut and we get 50, now that is noticeably different, chances are you will see some fireworks going off within the market.

The CPI: The Consumer Price Index is a measure of the average price of a fixed basket of goods and services. In plain terms we are taking a look at the rate of inflation. Why do we care about this? In the US it is definitely one of the most watched indicators of inflation. Outside of the US, whether it is in Europe, Asia, or elsewhere their particular CPI is watched very closely by the market and it will influence how interest rates are set on loans, mortgages, bonds, etc.

Nonfarm Payrolls: One of the biggest reports for traders. It gives the number of employees working in US businesses. Non-agricultural jobs, hence non-farm. Why do we care? It gives a comprehensive picture of how many people are working, looking for work, how much they make, basically a snapshot of the job market within the United States.

Housing Starts: Measures the initial construction of single-multi family homes each month. Why do we care? In two words, the ripple effect! The market pays attention to housing starts whether it is in the States or elsewhere because of this ripple effect. Building homes, 10, 20 homes, an apartment complex, it ripples throughout the economy. You will see examples of this with the employment of persons to build the homes, furniture for those homes, utilities, and even with trade because materials may need to be imported to build those homes. Clearly, these ripples are noticeable and economists pay very close attention to housing start numbers.

CHAPTER 5

TECHNICAL ANALYSIS QUICK TRADE GUIDE

Chart Time Frame

Time frame, the most critical factor of a trading decision. The decision to buy or sell <u>always</u> begins with the time frame. A signal to buy or sell for a day trader is different from a swing trader and in most cases extremely different from a long term trader/investor. The examples we will use are based on short term/day trading time frames.

Day trading - Closing positions within 24 hours

Swing trading - Holding trades open from a few hours to maximum a few days

For short term traders a chart setting of 1 hour is good for getting a market overview, and then making the decision to trade off the 30 or 15 minutes chart. The shorter your trading time horizon the shorter you chart time frame.

Tip: One of the many benefits you will enjoy as you use multiple timeframes in your trading is that you will see the forex market from the perspectives of many different types of traders. By looking at both short-term and longer-term charts you will be aware of what both short-term and longer-term traders are watching. This will help to prevent you from being caught off-guard by any sudden price movements

When using the settings above it's recommended that you create charts of the different time frames and leave them open on your trading platform. This will make it more efficient to trade.

Time frame & your location in the buy - sell channel

Once the time frame has been set, you need to locate where you are in the buy-sell trade channel (the trade channel is the area between the high and low bands of the Bollinger Bands). If you are near the top of the channel that indicates that you are close to a potential reversal level (where the market turns/reverses), ex. if heading up, it suddenly heads down. If at the bottom and the market heads up it's also a reversal level.

What to do at reversal levels

This is where trading gets a bit tricky. Just because we are at or near a reversal level it's no guarantee that it will reverse. We could also get a breakout (the market going above/below known resistance or support levels). One tip in figuring out what to do next, is to simply review the chart for past market movements (did it go up or down) at the price level you are looking at. This is to see what happened in the market the last time the price was there. This is important because the central "person" here is the market not you). For example, if the market headed down then there is a good chance that it will do that again. However this is NOT a guarantee, and you also need to be aware of fundamental data (news report, economic data) as this could throw everything off from the result of the last time.

If you don't have a position open already, and the market is at a potential reversal level, one way to trade it is by setting a buy order above the reversal level. Therefore if the market does get the breakout then you are in. The buy order is also part of your risk management because there is only money on the table if it gets executed and becomes a trade.

After figuring out where you are in the buy-sell channel you now want to pay attention to the RSI and what it is telling you. You need to have a match between that and your trade execution. If the RSI is at overbought levels and you are near reversal levels on the Bollinger bands then it is a sign of a good potential sell opportunity.

Ideal buy signals

Ideally on a buy signal you want your RSI to be heading up from at or near the 30-40 levels giving good room/opportunity to head up. At the same time you also want the market to be located/trading near the bottom of the channel in the Bollinger Bands.

Finally, if using candle stick charts you will want them to be green (prices closing up). As you can see we need to see the same data(up) from our tools. Looking at red candle sticks(prices closing lower) and overbought (excessive buying) RSI levels is a mixed signal. This tell you to "stand aside"… do not trade until things are clearer.

Ideal sell signals

An ideal sell signal is simply the opposite of the above. In other words, your RSI will be heading <u>down</u> from 70-80 levels. At the same time you also want the market to be located/trading near the top of the channel in the Bollinger Bands. Finally, if using candle stick charts you will want them to be red (prices closing down).

Wrapping up

Ideally you want to execute a trade from when things are as close to ideal as possible. When faced with grey areas/undecided I suggest that you use buy or sell stop orders. Orders are NOT trades so no money is at risk until they are executed. These orders will be placed near the ideal levels that you are seeking to trade from. As I have stressed several times, ideal trade scenario or not, you always place a stop order. Unfortunately, even the world's best research is no guarantee of a profitable trade.

Settings for the technical analysis indicators

RSI

On RSI, the default of 14 is fine for most FX, CFD, equity trading. However with shorter term trading, day trading or swing trading then 14 is not optimal. I suggest 7 for swing trading and down to 4 for day trading.

Bollinger Bands

The default settings (20:2) seems to work best for most traders and I suggest that you keep this setting.

Moving Averages

We use 50, 100, 200. The 50 is the alert signal, 100 short term and 200 is the long term.

CHAPTER 6

TRADING TACTICS

Let us have a look at the five major reasons of traders' losses:

1. Unrealistic expectations, an example of this could be that you have one thousand Euros in your account and you expect to have two thousand in a day or maybe even at the end of the week.

2. No plan, as some say, "failing to plan is planning to fail." From my experience, plus I have spoken to many new traders in the past and what I heard after I asked them, "why did you place this trade?" would surprise many. I have heard "no idea", or mumbling about that a family member said it was a good thing to do, not exactly the best strategy.

3. Too much risk, this usually involves using your maximum leverage that's available.

4. Confusing trading with investing, two complete different things, trading is more technical analysis heavy, investing you are lean more heavily on fundamental analysis

principles. For example, with investing you have a time frame typically of three to five years, clearly fundamental issues are more important. If you are trading where it is minutes, maybe five, as far as the holding time then technical analysis will be the driver of your analysis.

5. Over and undertrading this we will take a look at a bit later.

Some solutions

Using low leverage is key because it ensures that a bad day of trading doesn't wipe out all of your profits. Then you must observe the traders golden rule, "no cash no trading", they are not too many ways to spin this, if there is no money there is no trading, so you do want to hold onto the cash. Next is scaling in scaling out, here you allow the market to speak to you. Yes, prior to any trade, you will do your analysis but after you have done your analysis you do allow the market to speak to you. Meaning that if you buy at one hundred and the market falls to ninety, it is telling you something, you need to lower your exposure. If you buy at one hundred and it goes to one hundred ten, one hundred twenty it is also telling you something, now you can consider additional market exposure.

In foreign exchange, select out a few pairs and get to know them well. It is not necessary to be an expert on twenty pairs or fifteen, the bottom line remains the bottom line, which is to make money. It is not a competition on how many pairs you know, even if you are doing electronic or algo trading in many cases it is still pretty specific that you are focusing on five or six different pairs and not much more than that.

Many people ask about what are the good pairs for trading and I suggest that Eurodollar, Dollaryen, Cable, Dollarswiss are good places to begin. With these pairs it would not be an exceptional event to see a one hundred pips move or more. One of the main points with trading is that you need and want to see movements. If you have placed a trade and nothing happens, after you already paid the spread, then you have given a gift to your broker or bank, so you do want to go where the action is. Of the pairs mentioned, when trying to decide on the best one, you want to check on the spreads and clearly the ones with the tightest spreads, your cost of doing business, will have an edge. This is basic, the cheaper it is for you to trade, the easier it is for you to make money. There are not too many ways to get around this, you do want to focus on the pairs that cost the least amount to trade.

In CFDs and stock, company upgrades, profit warnings are good opportunities to trade for quick profits. The prices tend to go in the direction of the announcement. For example, your favorite company is unable to meet their quarterly earnings estimate, then chances are that stock will fall and you can look into opening a short position.

When trading, the winners and the losers, they reveal themselves pretty quickly and you do want to remove the losers as soon as possible. Your stop loss with forex is usually fifteen, twenty, or twenty-five pips depending on your risk profile. To be very clear about this point, I'm referring to *trading*, not investing. If you open an investment position where you are looking at three years, five years, then yes if you are not making money that first day or that first week, nothing to panic over, but if you are trading with a time frame of a minute, five minutes, a day, then a different story. With trading you do want to remove the losers as soon as possible.

Next you want to have a trade plan, with your stop levels, profit levels, correct amounts and pairs all set. It sounds basic, but yes if you are attempting to trade Eurodollar you really should trade Eurodollar. The term is called "fat fingers" which occurs unfortunately on a daily basis, you want to trade Eurodollar you type in Euroyen, you want to trade British Airways, you type in British Aerospace, it goes on far too often. With that in mind, remain alert with your trading so that the correct thing is keyed in when executing.

News trading

News trading, this is an opportunity where you get to trade without paying attention to anyone. A little bit of danger, slippage, this can wipe out all of your profits. Slippage simply means that you buy at one hundred and you have a stop loss at ninety, instead of getting out at ninety, it could be eighty-five, eighty or lower.

To set up a news trade, roughly half hour before the event, you want to use relatively tight chart settings (15 min to 30 min) because this is aggressive trading. For your entry, a few pips above where we are trading (at that moment) place a buy stop order. A few pips beneath place a sell stop order. You can also use the resistance levels and support levels as guidance, depending on your risk profile, you can just place a buy stop order twenty pips above and a sell stop order twenty pips beneath.

The exit point is typically the size of the range. For example, if the range is thirty pips, you can use that as your initial profit taking or limit order. Some traders just use if they are long, a twenty pips stop loss and then take profit at one hundred, one hundred twenty pips depending again on the person's risk exposure and profile. There is some room to play with this, if you are in a position and you are making a profit you don't need to take it all at once, you can scale out of it gradually.

Solutions: Undertraders and Overtraders

Returning to our undertraders and overtraders. Overtraders don't know when to stop, they try to get everything out of the market. Undertraders they obey the 2 % rule but they stop as they have a little profit. Reading between the lines you are basically looking at greed and fear. That 2 % rule, by the way, states that you should not risk more than 2% of an account balance on any one trade. Here you can play with it a little bit, 3%, 4%, maybe even up to 5% that's ok, but beyond that you are breaking out of the guideline. The point of this is that when you are using this 2, or 3 or 4 % you are *making failure survivable*. In other words, you can be wrong a lot and still continue trading.

Some solutions to over-under trading: you set a daily profit target, overtrader stop once they get there, the undertrader needs to keep going, and then obviously everyone stops once the daily loss limit is reached, no negotiations. Finally, if your technical or fundamental analysis data is unclear or as I call it messy you do have the right not to trade.

CHAPTER 7

TRANSITION FROM DEMO TO LIVE TRADING

This is a topic that is of concern and interest for many of my students and I would say a lot of demo traders in general. How do you go from the situation where you have a demo account into one that is funded, where you have actually placed money on the account.

There are a few steps: First, is that you do need to work with what I call a realistic account balance. This implies that if you are planning to begin trading with five thousand Euros, two thousand Euros, or ten thousand, the amount is not so critical, what is critical and important is that it matches your intended opening balance. If you plan to start with five thousand Euros, then your demo balance needs to match this.

What I have personally seen in the past with new traders is that they have gone through the demo experience using the default demo balance on many platforms. These balances are usually somewhere between a hundred thousand Euros or a couple hundred thousand Euros, and the person does a lot of demo trading on one hundred thousand, two hundred thousand, then they open an account with ten thousand Euros, maybe twenty thousand Euros or five thousand Euros. Nothing wrong with these amounts, because obviously ten thousand, even five thousand Euros, it is money, it is something, but the challenge they face is they never practiced on those amounts. They were using the defaults of one hundred thousand, a couple hundred thousand and they didn't internalize this. With internalize I mean that when you are trading, you need to know how it feels to earn or lose on the intended opening balance. Whether it is five thousand or ten thousand you need to actually experience it mentally and in some ways physically in your body trading on the balance. Once you have gone through this, when it is time to switch to a live account, I promise you that you will not be able to tell the difference. This is because you have practiced on this amount with gains and losses and you know how it feels so that when you go to the live account it is like wow! the live account is pretty much like you gone through on the demo which is the point.

From here the next step is using realistic or expected trading sizes. If you have a five thousand, ten thousand Euros opening account balance, then the position sizes need to be fifty thousand, a hundred thousand, maybe a couple hundred thousand. Those amounts are realistic for those balances to avoid that you are not placing trades of ten million, twenty million, when you know that is not something you will normally do. Of course, if you are in that situation then fine, then you can have trades of five and ten million but that really isn't the norm for new traders.

To complete the transition to a funded account, obviously you need to have a consistent plus on your demo account balance. When you are trading you don't need to make money every day, but at the end of the week or in general you should end up in the black, in the plus, that you are making money. If you aren't making any money in demo trading then that is telling you that you need to demo trade some more.

To recap, first and I would say by far the most important is that you do have this realistic account balance, so that you actually know how you will react mentally and physically to gains or losses, realistic trade sizes, and you do need to be making a consistent profit in your account.

CHAPTER 8

SELECTING A TRADE PARTNER

What is it you that look for when you are considering opening a funded trading account? First, a reliable platform, for me reliable means that when it's time to trade the platform is working, also meaning that you can get steaming (tradable) prices which allows you to buy and sell with ease. If you are trading with a broker that has a platform that is down more than a couple times a year, then you definitely want to consider switching, it really shouldn't be that they are down more than maybe once a year, because most platforms are up all the time.

Next thing you want to look at is what I call good liquidity over numbers. When I mention "numbers" I am referring to if you are looking to do news trading over job reports, interest rate reports, housing numbers, etc. There are many traders where more or less a lot of their strategy is based on trading as we call it in the business, "over numbers." This is trading in the middle of market news reports and this is also the time when you can actually get into this situation of a liquidity squeeze. In a concrete example with needing good liquidity over numbers, let us say that the Bank of England rate decision is announced, you are attempting a trade, and when you try to buy or sell your broker keeps requoting the prices or maybe they won't even allow you to execute. If you are experiencing this on a regular basis, you should consider trading elsewhere because you should be able to get trading done even over news reports.

Finally, you definitely want to speak to your friends, if you have a friend who is an active trader, find out about his experiences with his broker. Because usually this a good source of how they (the broker) are when you need to trade. You will also want to know about the process when there is a need to transfer money to the account or from the account. What has been your friend's experience? has it been pretty smooth or has there been a lot of administration and they needed to send many emails in order to accomplish this.

In review of the things that you need in selecting a good trading partner, a reliable platform, good liquidity over market reports, and feedback from your friends.

CONCLUSION

Thank you for making it through to the end of *Technical Analysis for Forex Explained*. Let's hope it was informative and able to provide you with the first set of tools that you need to achieve your goals of trading using technical analysis with forex and making money with it.

The next step is to test your skills at trading and build up your risk capital so that you can make additional trades. This will give you the motivation that you need to succeed.

I have several other books on different aspects of trading and asset classes please check them out!

PROFILE OF THE AUTHOR

Wayne Walker is the director of a global capital markets education and consulting firm (gcmsonline.info). He has several years experience in leading and coaching teams of Investment Advisors and has managed top performing teams in the Private Client Group based on Bench Mark Earnings (BME).

www.ingramcontent.com/pod-product-compliance
Lightning Source LLC
Chambersburg PA
CBHW061448180526
45170CB00004B/1614